Budgeting for Black Friday

Budgeting for Black Friday

Matthew Petchinsky

1

Budgeting for Black Friday: A Holiday Savings Planner
By: Matthew Petchinsky

Introduction: The Calm Before the Cart—Mastering the Art of Guilt-Free Black Friday Shopping

Every November, the world braces for a retail storm known as **Black Friday**—a day when prices drop, adrenaline surges, and logic can easily take a back seat to temptation. Shoppers set alarms before dawn, refresh online carts with nervous excitement, and race through aisles in pursuit of the "deal of the year." But behind the glossy banners of *70% off* and *limited-time savings* lies a quieter reality: overspending, financial regret, and post-purchase guilt.

The Risks of Overspending During Black Friday

Black Friday is a carefully designed psychological playground for impulsive spending. Retailers use scarcity tactics—*"only 3 left in stock!"*—to trigger fear of missing out, while time-limited offers create the illusion that every purchase is urgent and essential. The danger is not the deals themselves, but the emotional rush they create. In the heat of excitement, it becomes alarmingly easy to justify purchases outside your budget, leading to debt accumulation that lingers long after the holiday lights fade.

Overspending during Black Friday doesn't always feel reckless in the moment. A single "small splurge" here and there accumulates quietly, especially when spread across multiple transactions and digital wallets. By the time the weekend transitions into Cyber Monday, many shoppers realize they've exceeded their intended budget by hundreds—sometimes thousands—of dollars. This post-shopping guilt can sour the holiday experience, creating anxiety that overshadows the joy of giving.

How Planning Ensures Guilt-Free Shopping

The antidote to overspending is not avoidance—it's **intention**. *Budgeting for Black Friday: A Holiday Savings Planner* transforms shopping chaos into a mindful, strategic process that safeguards your finances while letting you fully enjoy the excitement of holiday deals.

This planner helps you approach Black Friday with a game plan rather than guesswork. By setting clear spending limits, identifying your *true priorities*, and tracking every purchase, you transform shopping from a reactive experience into a controlled, empowering act of decision-making. Instead of falling victim to impulse buys, you'll navigate sales with confidence, knowing exactly where your money is going—and why.

Planning doesn't restrict joy; it enhances it. Every purchase you make within your plan becomes guilt-free because it aligns with your goals and values. You'll experience the thrill of saving without the dread of debt, and your post-Black Friday reflection will be one of satisfaction, not remorse.

As you move through this planner, you'll find tools, prompts, and templates designed to make financial discipline effortless and engaging. You'll learn how to allocate your resources wisely, spot psychological traps used by retailers, and even prepare for next year's deals with smarter foresight.

Black Friday doesn't have to be a financial battlefield—it can be a test of clarity, self-mastery, and abundance consciousness. With this planner as your guide, you'll shop smarter, spend intentionally, and emerge from the holiday season not with regret, but with gratitude—for your savings, your discipline, and your peace of mind.

Chapter 1: Setting a Realistic Shopping Budget

The Power of a Plan Before the Purchase

Before the shopping carts roll and the digital wish lists expand, the most powerful financial move you can make is establishing a **realistic, intentional budget**. Your budget is not just a spreadsheet of numbers—it's a roadmap that defines what matters most to you during the holiday season. It transforms chaotic spending into a deliberate act of alignment between your values and your wallet.

Setting a realistic budget means confronting three key realities:

1. How much you can safely spend without destabilizing your financial health.
2. What purchases will truly bring value or joy beyond the short-term thrill.
3. How to balance emotional desires with practical needs.

When approached correctly, your Black Friday budget becomes a shield—protecting your savings, preventing overspending, and empowering you to shop confidently, knowing you are in full control.

Step 1: Understanding Your Financial Baseline

Start by identifying your **financial baseline**, the amount of money available to spend after accounting for non-negotiable expenses. This includes rent or mortgage, utilities, insurance, transportation, groceries, and debt payments. Subtract these essentials from your monthly income to reveal your *discretionary spending limit*—the maximum safe amount available for shopping.

If your income fluctuates or you rely on gig work, calculate your **three-month average income** to create a stable reference point. This prevents budgeting based on optimistic or temporary earnings highs. Remember: a realistic budget is built on facts, not hopes.

Tip: Use the 50/30/20 rule as a flexible guide—

- **50%** of income covers needs
- **30%** covers wants (where holiday spending fits)
- **20%** goes to savings or debt repayment

Your Black Friday shopping should fit neatly within that 30% zone, never bleeding into essentials or emergency funds.

Step 2: Identifying Spending Priorities

Every sale claims to be "can't-miss," but not all purchases carry equal weight. Start by dividing your potential buys into **priority categories**:

1. **Gifts** – Family, friends, or coworkers you plan to buy for.
2. **Household Needs** – Appliances, furniture, or electronics that truly need upgrading.
3. **Personal Indulgences** – Items that bring you joy or comfort (but not at the cost of guilt).
4. **Future Investments** – Tools, education, or technology that improve your productivity or well-being.

Once you've listed your categories, assign a **percentage of your total budget** to each one. For instance:

- Gifts: 40%
- Household: 25%
- Personal: 20%
- Investments: 15%

This system helps you visualize where your money will have the most impact and keeps you from splurging impulsively in one area.

Step 3: Accounting for Hidden Costs

Black Friday deals often come with **hidden financial traps** that erode your budget without notice. Common culprits include:

- **Taxes and shipping fees** – Many discounts appear smaller once these are added at checkout.
- **Add-on warranties** – Usually unnecessary, they quietly inflate costs.
- **Subscription trials** – "Free" offers that charge later if forgotten.
- **Impulse extras** – Accessories, cables, or "complete the bundle" upsells.

Build a **10–15% buffer** into your budget to cover these invisible expenses. If you end up not using it, that buffer becomes your post-holiday savings win.

Step 4: Creating Spending Limits Per Store or Category

Divide your total budget into **store-specific or category-based limits**. For example:

- Amazon: $200
- Target: $150
- Best Buy: $100
- Clothing: $80
- Home Décor: $70

This segmentation ensures you never get carried away by one retailer's marketing or by "doorbuster" hype. You'll know exactly how much freedom you have before crossing the threshold—virtual or physical.

Bonus Strategy: Use prepaid debit cards or digital wallets preloaded with your designated spending amount. Once it's gone, it's gone—creating a natural stopping point that protects you from overspending.

Step 5: The Emotional Check-In — Knowing Your "Why"
Budgets aren't just about numbers—they're about **motivation**. Before finalizing your spending plan, take a moment to ask:

- Why am I buying this item?
- Does it fulfill a genuine need, or is it filling an emotional void?
- Will this purchase still feel worthwhile in January?

Emotional awareness prevents "stress spending" and helps you reframe shopping as a mindful, rewarding activity rather than an escape. When you shop with emotional clarity, every transaction supports your happiness rather than hijacking it.

Step 6: Building Flexibility Into Your Budget

Rigid budgets often fail because life—and sales—don't always go according to plan. A **flexible budget** keeps you steady when priorities shift. If you find a necessary item on deeper discount than expected, it's okay to reallocate funds, as long as total spending doesn't exceed your limit.

Treat your budget as a **living document**, not a locked cage. You are free to adapt, revise, and improve as deals unfold—so long as you remain aligned with your larger goal: staying financially empowered and guilt-free.

Step 7: The Final Budget Check

Before shopping begins, perform a final audit of your plan:

- ◈ Essential bills paid and current?
- ◈ Emergency fund untouched?
- ◈ Budget categories defined and realistic?
- ◈ Spending buffer included?
- ◈ Emotional motives checked?

If all are confirmed, you are ready to approach Black Friday not as a consumer swept up by chaos—but as a **strategic buyer** with control, foresight, and confidence.

Closing Reflection: Abundance Through Awareness

True abundance doesn't come from buying more—it comes from **feeling secure in what you choose to buy**. By setting a realistic shopping budget, you are creating peace of mind as your greatest purchase this season. Every dollar you direct with intention becomes a symbol of self-respect and empowerment.

Chapter 2: Prioritizing Wants vs. Needs

The Psychology of Holiday Temptation

Black Friday is designed to blur the line between what you **want** and what you **need**. Retailers create emotional urgency through flashing banners, countdown timers, and phrases like *"Only 2 left!"* or *"You deserve this."* These messages appeal not to logic—but to **impulse and emotion**. When dopamine surges at the thought of scoring a "limited deal," it becomes easy to convince yourself that the new tablet, shoes, or kitchen gadget is essential.

To make smart, guilt-free decisions, you must reclaim your awareness. Prioritizing wants vs. needs is not about depriving yourself—it's about developing **financial mindfulness**. It's learning to pause before purchase and ask, "Is this something that will genuinely improve my life, or something that will only excite me temporarily?"

By mastering this skill, you'll turn every shopping choice into a conscious act of alignment rather than a reaction to pressure.

Step 1: Define What a "Need" Truly Is

A **need** is something that serves a direct, lasting purpose in your well-being, productivity, or survival. It's a purchase that either:

- Replaces something broken or outdated that you regularly use.
- Improves safety, health, or long-term efficiency.
- Fulfills a real obligation (like a gift for family or tools for work).

Examples of genuine Black Friday needs might include:

- A discounted laptop you rely on for work or study.
- Winter clothing to replace worn-out essentials.
- A reliable set of kitchen appliances for meal preparation.

Needs tend to **retain value** long after the excitement fades. They are practical investments that enhance your daily life.

Step 2: Identify What Falls Into the "Want" Category

A **want**, by contrast, is emotionally driven. It's something that *adds pleasure* but isn't vital for your current stability. Wants are not inherently bad—they're part of enjoying life—but they must be managed consciously to avoid financial guilt later.

Common examples of wants during Black Friday include:

- Buying the newest version of an item you already own.
- Purchasing luxury upgrades purely for status or novelty.
- Impulse "self-care" items that aren't planned (extra candles, décor, or designer clothes).

Wants are often tied to **mood-based spending**—a response to stress, fatigue, or social pressure rather than true necessity. Recognizing them in the moment allows you to slow down and decide if the short-term joy is worth the long-term cost.

Step 3: The 3-Question Filter

Before any purchase, apply this quick but powerful filter:

1. **Will this item improve or simplify my life for more than 6 months?**
   - If yes, it may be a *need*.
2. **Would I still want this if it weren't on sale?**
   - If no, it's likely a *want*.
3. **Am I buying this because I planned to—or because it's in front of me?**
   - If the latter, you're reacting to marketing, not strategy.

Write these questions on a sticky note and place it near your computer or wallet during Black Friday weekend. That tiny pause of reflection can save hundreds of dollars—and countless hours of regret.

Step 4: Ranking Your Shopping List

Once you've separated your wants and needs, create a **ranking system** to determine purchase order and importance.

Example System:

- **Tier 1: Essential Needs (Buy First)**
  - Items crucial to functionality, safety, or obligations.
  - Example: Work electronics, home maintenance tools, necessary clothing.
- **Tier 2: Supportive Needs (Buy If Budget Allows)**
  - Items that enhance comfort or efficiency but aren't urgent.
  - Example: Organizational tools, upgraded cookware, practical home décor.
- **Tier 3: Meaningful Wants (Buy Last)**
  - Items that bring joy or personal reward but have no functional necessity.
  - Example: Luxury candles, hobby accessories, new headphones when the old ones work fine.
- **Tier 4: Impulse Wants (Avoid or Delay)**
  - Items not on your list or influenced by sudden emotion.
  - Example: Mystery boxes, extra "buy-one-get-one" deals, unplanned tech upgrades.

This hierarchy helps you navigate deals rationally. You'll know exactly where to draw the line once funds begin to run low.

Step 5: The Emotional Audit

Every financial decision is also an emotional one. Before you click "checkout," ask yourself:

- *Am I tired, anxious, or trying to reward myself for stress?*
- *Am I comparing myself to others on social media?*
- *Would I buy this if no one else could see it?*

These reflections reveal whether you're shopping to fill a psychological gap rather than a practical one. Emotional awareness converts consumer reflex into self-awareness—a major win during high-pressure sales events.

You may also notice patterns. For instance:

- Buying electronics for a sense of control.
- Purchasing beauty products for self-worth validation.
- Collecting items as comfort during uncertainty.

Recognizing these habits lets you redirect that emotional energy into meaningful rewards—such as setting aside money for travel, personal growth, or experiences that bring lasting joy.

Step 6: Balancing Reward and Responsibility

A balanced approach to Black Friday shopping acknowledges both **desire and discipline**. You don't need to strip yourself of joy to stay financially secure—you simply need to integrate both worlds.

Consider setting up a **"reward allowance"** within your budget:

- Allocate 10–15% of your total spending limit for guilt-free wants.
- Label it your "holiday joy fund."
- Once it's used, stop.

This ensures you can indulge without guilt while maintaining long-term control. It also transforms wants from sources of stress into symbols of balance and self-trust.

Step 7: Using Visualization to Clarify Value

Before finalizing any purchase, imagine your **future self** holding the item 30 days later.

- Does it still feel necessary?
- Does it still excite you?
- Has it genuinely improved your life, or is it collecting dust?

Visualization connects you to the long-term value of your decision, grounding your choices in foresight instead of adrenaline.

You can also use a "cooling-off period" for wants—wait 24 hours before buying. If you forget about the item or lose interest, it wasn't meant to be. If you still want it the next day, it may be worth it.

Step 8: Practical Tools for Prioritization
Use your planner to organize purchases visually:

Category	Item	Priority (1–4)	Planned Budget	Actual Cost	Keep or Pass
Electronics	Laptop upgrade	1	$300		
Clothing	Winter coat	2	$120		
Décor	Holiday candles	3	$25		
Misc	Random gadgets	4	$0		

This table gives you a real-time overview of how your spending aligns with your priorities. You can quickly see where adjustments are needed before any damage is done.

Step 9: Turning Needs Into Investments

When you spend on needs, think beyond survival—think **return on investment (ROI)**. Ask:

- Will this save me money or time in the long run?
- Will it prevent a future repair or replacement?
- Will it improve my earning potential or daily well-being?

By reframing needs as investments, you anchor your shopping in value rather than reaction. Each purchase becomes part of your larger wealth and well-being strategy.

Step 10: Reflecting After the Purchase

Once Black Friday ends, review your receipts and note how each purchase made you feel. Did it provide relief, satisfaction, or regret? This post-purchase reflection teaches you where your discipline held strong and where your emotional triggers took over.

The next shopping event will feel easier because you'll already understand your personal spending psychology.

Closing Reflection: Choosing Intention Over Impulse

Distinguishing between wants and needs is the foundation of **conscious spending**. Every time you make a choice rooted in awareness, you're declaring financial sovereignty. You're no longer reacting to sales—you're commanding them.

As you move forward, remember: joy doesn't come from the volume of items you own, but from the peace that comes with knowing you spent wisely and intentionally.

Chapter 3: Creating Smart Shopping Lists

The Power of the List: Why It's Your Greatest Weapon

Every year, millions of shoppers enter Black Friday with the best intentions and leave with overflowing carts, drained accounts, and a haze of confusion about where their money went. The difference between those who *save strategically* and those who *spend impulsively* often comes down to one thing: **the list**.

A well-crafted shopping list is not merely a set of reminders — it's a **financial compass** that keeps you anchored when the marketing waves start crashing. It helps you differentiate genuine opportunities from distractions, ensuring that every item you purchase serves a defined purpose in your life or holiday goals.

Without a list, sales dictate your behavior. With one, you dictate your strategy.

Step 1: Start with Reflection — What Went Right (and Wrong) Last Year

Before you jot down a single product, take 10 minutes to reflect on your **past shopping experiences**. Ask yourself:

- What purchases from last year still bring me value today?
- Which ones caused regret or went unused?
- Did I overspend in one area (like tech or décor) and neglect another (like gifts or essentials)?

This reflection phase gives you data-driven insight into your habits. By analyzing last year's wins and losses, you can correct patterns of overspending and redirect your energy toward smarter, more rewarding buys.

If this is your first year using a planner like *Budgeting for Black Friday*, treat this step as an opportunity to define your **shopping identity**. Are you a practical buyer, a generous gift-giver, or a spontaneous deal-hunter? Knowing your tendencies helps you craft a list that aligns with your strengths — not your impulses.

Step 2: Clarify Your Shopping Goals

Every purchase should serve a **goal**, not just a desire. Write down what you hope to achieve this Black Friday in one to three sentences. For example:

- "I want to buy thoughtful, affordable gifts for my family without dipping into savings."
- "I want to upgrade key home electronics within a set budget of $600."
- "I want to enjoy shopping without debt, regret, or post-holiday stress."

Your goals act as emotional anchors. When you feel tempted by an unplanned deal, you can look back at your list and ask, "Does this serve my original goal?" If not, it doesn't belong in your cart.

Step 3: Divide Your List into Core Categories

Organizing your list into categories ensures you see your spending at a glance and prevents one area from dominating your budget. Use the following foundational structure:

1. **Gifts** – Items for family, friends, coworkers, or charitable giving.
2. **Home & Household** – Appliances, décor, bedding, or essential upgrades.
3. **Personal Items** – Clothing, accessories, self-care, or personal tech.
4. **Work & Productivity** – Office supplies, digital tools, or educational investments.
5. **Future Planning** – Items that contribute to long-term goals (health, skill-building, etc.).

You can also create custom categories like "Pet Supplies," "Holiday Décor," or "Experiences" depending on your lifestyle.

Pro Tip: Add a small "Wishlist" category at the end — this gives you a safe space for optional wants without derailing your main budget.

Step 4: Assign Budgets to Each Category

After defining your categories, assign each one a **spending limit** based on importance and available funds. Use your total budget from Chapter 1 as a guide.

For instance:

Category	Budget Limit	% of Total	Priority Level
Gifts	$300	40%	High
Home & Household	$200	25%	Medium
Personal	$150	20%	Medium
Work & Productivity	$100	10%	Medium
Wishlist	$50	5%	Low

Setting limits creates accountability. It prevents the emotional “spillover effect,” where savings in one category become justification for splurging elsewhere.

Step 5: Research and Pre-Select Specific Items

The smartest shoppers don't wait for the sales to begin — they prepare in advance. Research your desired items **weeks before Black Friday** to understand normal pricing trends. This ensures you can recognize *real* discounts instead of deceptive markdowns.

For each item, note:

- Regular price
- Target sale price
- Retailers offering it
- Alternative brands or models

Example:

Item	Regular Price	Target Sale Price	Retailers	Notes
Noise-canceling headphones	$299	$199	Best Buy, Amazon	Only if under $200
Air fryer	$120	$80	Target, Walmart	Check warranty
Winter jacket	$180	$100	Macy's	Replace old coat

This table functions as your *battle plan*. When the sales begin, you already know what a good deal looks like — removing the guesswork and emotional rush that often leads to regret.

Step 6: Use the "Need-Want Filter"

Cross-reference your list with the principles from Chapter 2. Label each item as **Need** or **Want**.

- **Needs**: Buy early or secure during first-wave sales.
- **Wants**: Delay until Cyber Monday or end-of-day flash sales, when discounts deepen.

Color-coding or symbol systems (� for needs, � for wants) help you visually track which items are essential versus optional.

Step 7: Rank Your Items by Priority and Urgency

Not all items are created equal — even among your needs. Rank your list in descending order of importance to make quick decisions if sales overlap or stock runs out.

Example Priority Tiers:

- **Tier 1 – Essential Now:** Must-buy items that fulfill immediate needs or rare opportunities.
- **Tier 2 – Valuable Soon:** Helpful items that can wait for the right deal.
- **Tier 3 – Optional Later:** Desirable, non-essential items that can be postponed or skipped.

Having a ranked list prevents panic spending. If your top priority item sells out, you can move to the next one without spiraling into impulse buying.

Step 8: Consider Timing and Availability

Many retailers stagger their discounts throughout **Black Friday Week** and **Cyber Monday**, so mapping your list by timing ensures strategic execution.

- **Early Bird Deals (Pre-Black Friday):** Good for essential household items or early gifts.
- **Black Friday Doorbusters:** Ideal for electronics and big-ticket upgrades.
- **Cyber Monday:** Best for online exclusives, software, or subscription-based items.
- **Post-Black Friday Clearance:** Perfect for décor, apparel, and accessories.

Planning purchases across these phases stretches your budget further and prevents burnout from doing all your shopping at once.

Step 9: Use Tools and Apps for Smarter Tracking

Modern shoppers have an advantage: **technology that prevents overspending**. Use apps and browser extensions that alert you to price drops, apply coupon codes, or compare sellers automatically.

Some popular options include:

- **Honey** – Auto-applies the best coupon at checkout.
- **CamelCamelCamel** – Tracks Amazon price history.
- **Rakuten (Ebates)** – Offers cash back for online purchases.
- **Google Shopping** – Compares item prices across multiple retailers instantly.

Integrating these tools into your planner ensures that your list evolves dynamically with real-time opportunities.

Step 10: Include Non-Material Goals

A truly smart shopping list goes beyond products — it includes **intentions**. Add a short section for non-material objectives such as:

- "Stay under budget by 15%."
- "Donate one item for every three purchased."
- "Finish shopping before noon to avoid stress."

These goals turn your shopping day into a purposeful ritual rather than a chaotic marathon.

Step 11: Review, Edit, and Finalize

Before Black Friday officially begins, review your entire list with a critical eye. Ask:

- Do these items still align with my goals?
- Have I researched all major retailers for better prices?
- Is there room left for unexpected opportunities?

Trim, rearrange, and polish your list until it reflects **clarity, balance, and focus**. Remember: every unnecessary item you remove increases the impact of the purchases that remain.

Step 12: Commit to the List — and Trust It

The final step is psychological: once your list is complete, **commit to it**. Shopping lists fail not because they're inaccurate, but because we abandon them in the heat of the moment.

Think of your list as a **binding contract with your future self** — one who values stability, savings, and peace of mind more than fleeting excitement. Each time temptation strikes, remind yourself: "If it's not on the list, it's not in the cart."

Closing Reflection: Lists as Anchors of Abundance

Creating a smart shopping list is not about restricting joy—it's about directing it. When your spending aligns with your priorities, every purchase becomes a celebration of awareness and discipline.

Your list is your proof that abundance is not chaos—it's **clarity**. It's the quiet satisfaction of knowing that every dollar you spent was a choice, not a reaction.

Chapter 4: Smart Deal Hunting Strategies

The Mindset of a Smart Deal Hunter

Black Friday isn't just a shopping event—it's a *psychological battlefield*. Retailers spend billions crafting limited-time offers that manipulate urgency and perception. Smart deal hunting requires shifting from emotional reaction to **strategic analysis**. The goal is no longer to "find the best deal," but to **verify** that a deal is actually *real* and aligns with your priorities.

A true deal hunter approaches Black Friday like a financial strategist:

- Researches before reacting.
- Compares before committing.
- Times purchases based on data, not hype.

In this chapter, you'll learn how to spot real value, filter marketing noise, and build a dynamic system that ensures your savings are genuine—not illusionary.

Step 1: Understanding How Retailers Create the Illusion of Savings

Before mastering deal hunting, you must recognize the most common **sales psychology traps** designed to override your logic:

1. **Price Anchoring:** A retailer lists a product's "original" price as artificially high, then slashes it to make the discount appear massive (e.g., "Was $499, now $199!"). In reality, the item may have sold for $199 all year.
2. **Scarcity Pressure:** Flashing countdown timers or "Only 3 left in stock!" banners create false urgency to make you act impulsively.
3. **Bundled Inflation:** Retailers package products together to disguise a small discount as a large one. Often, one or more included items aren't needed.
4. **Tiered Discounts:** "Buy 3 to get 20% off" encourages overspending on items you wouldn't have bought otherwise.
5. **Fake Limited Editions:** Some "exclusive" products are standard models with superficial tweaks or colors.

Awareness neutralizes these tactics. When you recognize manipulation in action, you regain control and can make your decisions from clarity, not adrenaline.

Step 2: Conducting Pre-Sale Price Research

Effective deal hunting begins *before* the sale starts. Retailers track customer behavior weeks in advance, so you must do the same. Create a **Pre-Sale Research Table** to record regular prices:

Item	Retailer	Regular Price	Desired Price	Notes
Smart TV 55"	Best Buy	$499	$349	Wait for Doorbuster or Cyber Monday
Air Purifier	Amazon	$180	$120	Track with price alerts
Coffee Maker	Walmart	$99	$75	Check bundle version—may include filters

Use tools like **CamelCamelCamel**, **Honey**, or **PriceRunner** to view **price history charts**. If a "deal" appears that's barely below the regular rate, you'll know it's not a true bargain.

Step 3: Building Your "Deal Watchlist"

Once your research is done, build a **Deal Watchlist**—a curated list of specific items you're monitoring across multiple platforms.

How to Build It:

1. Choose your top 10–15 high-value items.
2. Bookmark or save links in a single folder or spreadsheet.
3. Set up automated email or app alerts for price drops.
4. Record price fluctuations daily or weekly in your planner.

By centralizing all your deals in one place, you eliminate the scatter of jumping from site to site and reduce the emotional pull of random sales ads.

Step 4: Mastering Comparison Shopping

Comparison shopping is where the smart deal hunter thrives. Always cross-check across **at least three** retailers before clicking "buy."

Key comparison points:

- **Base price:** The actual cost before coupons or tax.
- **Shipping and warranty costs:** A free-shipping item may beat a "cheaper" one with hidden fees.
- **Return policy:** A slightly higher price from a store with free returns may be worth it.
- **Rewards programs:** Points, cash-back bonuses, or loyalty discounts can add invisible savings.

Example:

A $500 laptop at Store A might seem cheaper than $520 at Store B—but if Store B offers 10% cash-back and a $20 store credit, it's the smarter buy.

Step 5: Use Browser Extensions and Cashback Programs

Technology is your ally in deal verification. Install trusted extensions that do the work for you:

- **Honey**: Automatically tests promo codes at checkout.
- **Rakuten (Ebates)**: Gives cash-back on qualifying purchases.
- **Capital One Shopping**: Tracks real-time price changes and suggests cheaper sellers.
- **RetailMeNot**: Aggregates verified coupon codes and rebates.
- **Karma (formerly Shoptagr)**: Notifies you the instant a saved item drops in price.

Combine cashback with credit card reward programs for double value. If your credit card offers 2–5% back on purchases, pair it with Rakuten's 5% cashback to save 10% overall.

Step 6: Timing the Market — When to Buy What

Not every deal peaks on Black Friday itself. Retail discounts often follow a predictable **sale cycle**:

Day	Best For	Reason
Monday–Wednesday (Pre-Sale)	Household basics, small electronics	Early birds secure inventory before it sells out.
Black Friday (Friday)	Televisions, appliances, fashion, beauty	Doorbusters and short-lived inventory drops.
Saturday–Sunday (Weekend)	Toys, games, mid-tier electronics	Family-oriented discounts kick in.
Cyber Monday (Monday)	Software, laptops, digital subscriptions	Online-only offers and bundle discounts.
Post-Cyber Week (Tuesday–Friday)	Clearance apparel, décor, leftovers	Retailers liquidate unsold stock for deeper discounts.

Time-sensitive awareness lets you plan purchases for maximum impact without rushing.

Step 7: Stacking Deals and Maximizing Discounts

A "stacked deal" combines multiple savings layers for exponential results. Smart shoppers treat every purchase as a math puzzle:

Example of Stacking:

1. Sale Price: 25% off item.
2. Promo Code: Extra 10% off.
3. Cashback: 5% through Rakuten.
4. Credit Card Offer: 3% category bonus.

Combined, a $100 item drops to $63.75 — a 36% total savings.

Pro Tip: Always apply discounts in the correct order—promo codes first, then cashback or rewards activation.

Step 8: Watch for "Shadow Discounts" and Price Adjustments

Many retailers quietly offer **price adjustments** if an item you purchased drops in price within a few days. This is a powerful hidden tactic that can save you hundreds.

- Check each store's **price adjustment policy** before buying.
- Record purchase dates and prices in your planner.
- If a price drops, contact customer service for a refund or store credit.

Some credit cards, like American Express or Chase, also offer **purchase protection**, reimbursing the difference if a price lowers soon after.

Step 9: Avoid the "Deal Spiral"

One of the most common mistakes shoppers make is "chasing deals." This happens when you start browsing outside your prepared list because you've saved money elsewhere and feel justified to "reward" yourself.

Combat this with three techniques:

1. **The List Check** — If it's not on your official shopping list, skip it.
2. **The Pause Rule** — Wait 20 minutes before purchasing any unplanned item.
3. **The Total Tracker** — Keep your total spend visible at all times so you can see the impact of "just one more deal."

The best deal is *not* the cheapest—it's the one that supports your long-term goals and financial peace.

Step 10: Recognizing Real Value Beyond Discounts

A 70% discount on something you don't need is a **100% waste of money**. True value considers three dimensions:

1. **Longevity** – How long will it last?
2. **Use Frequency** – How often will you use it?
3. **Emotional Return** – Does it enrich your daily life, reduce stress, or improve your well-being?

When you evaluate every purchase through these filters, you'll find that even fewer deals result in greater satisfaction. You'll own less but enjoy more.

Step 11: Preparing for Lightning Deals and Flash Sales

Flash sales test your ability to stay calm under pressure. They typically last a few hours and sell out fast—but not every flash deal is a real steal.

Tactical Approach:

- Keep your pre-researched watchlist open.
- Use auto-fill for fast checkout.
- Only buy items that were *already on your list.*
- Double-check specs; some flash deals offer older or lower-tier models.

If you miss out on a lightning deal, don't panic. Retailers often restock or reissue similar offers later in the day or on Cyber Monday.

Step 12: Protecting Yourself from Scams and Counterfeits

The rise of online shopping has also brought a surge of fake retailers and counterfeit goods. Safeguard your wallet by:

- Only buying from **verified sellers** on platforms like Amazon (look for "Ships from and sold by Amazon.com").
- Avoiding links from unsolicited emails or social media ads.
- Using **secure payment methods** (credit cards or PayPal, not debit).
- Reading reviews—look for consistency in product descriptions and customer photos.

Your money's power is amplified when it's protected. Never sacrifice safety for the illusion of a deal.

Step 13: Keep a "Deal Log"

Document every major deal you commit to during the event. Record:

- Item name and store
- Date of purchase
- Original and discounted prices
- Discounts stacked
- Cashback or points earned
- Expected delivery date

This log becomes invaluable for tracking real savings (and essential for Chapter 5's "Tracking Purchases in Real Time").

Closing Reflection: The Hunter's Code of Clarity

Smart deal hunting is not about *chasing* every discount—it's about **choosing** the right ones. It's a discipline that rewards patience, awareness, and preparation.

When you plan, compare, and verify, you transform from a consumer into a strategist—someone who can enjoy the thrill of the hunt without falling prey to it.

Black Friday becomes less about chaos and more about control. You're not fighting for deals—you're mastering them.

Chapter 5: Tracking Purchases in Real Time

The Importance of Real-Time Tracking

Once the buying begins, even the best-laid budgets can unravel if you're not keeping a close eye on every transaction. Black Friday sales move fast, and with dozens of digital receipts, cashback offers, shipping confirmations, and preorders flooding your inbox, it's easy to lose track of what you've actually spent.

Real-time tracking is the bridge between strategy and discipline. It transforms your spending from an abstract guess into a concrete, measurable system that ensures you stay within budget and avoid post-shopping regret.

By building a live tracking system, you:

- Know exactly how much money remains in your spending budget.
- Prevent duplicate purchases or impulse buys.
- Confirm discounts and cashback are properly applied.
- Maintain organization for returns, refunds, and future budgeting.

In essence, tracking your purchases as they happen keeps your Black Friday experience efficient, empowering, and guilt-free.

Step 1: Centralize Your Tracking System

Scattered receipts and forgotten tabs lead to chaos. Before Black Friday begins, set up a **single, centralized hub** where every transaction will be recorded.

You can use any of the following:

- A dedicated **spreadsheet** (Google Sheets, Excel, or Notion).
- The **tracking templates** within your *Budgeting for Black Friday Planner*.
- A budgeting app like **YNAB, EveryDollar, or Mint**.
- A handwritten ledger if you prefer analog control.

The key is consistency — one place, updated frequently. Every purchase, refund, or pending transaction should flow into this system the moment it occurs.

Step 2: Create Your Real-Time Purchase Tracker Template

Here's a sample framework to help you organize information effectively:

Date	Store	Item	Category	Budgeted Amount	Actual Spent	Payment Method	Order Status	Cashback/ Points	Notes
11/28	Target	Air Fryer	Home	$80	$76.49	Credit	Shipped	5% Target Card	Used promo + coupon
11/29	Amazon	Bluetooth Earbuds	Gift	$60	$54.99	Debit	Delivered	2% Rakuten	Arrived early
11/29	Best Buy	Laptop	Work	$400	$389	Credit	Processing	3% Cashback	Watch for price drop

You can expand the sheet with columns for "Return Deadline" and "Warranty Expiration" to maintain complete oversight long after the sale ends.

Step 3: Update After Every Purchase

The most powerful part of real-time tracking is immediacy. As soon as a purchase is made—online or in-store—log it within **five minutes**.

Doing this immediately prevents "budget blindness," where you underestimate your total spending because you haven't seen the cumulative numbers.

If you're shopping online, set up browser extensions or email rules that automatically label and archive receipts into a folder named **Black Friday 2025**. This simplifies importing data later for review.

Step 4: Use Technology to Automate Monitoring

Automation prevents human error and saves valuable time. Consider integrating digital tools that connect directly to your bank or card accounts to update spending automatically:

- **Mint**: Syncs accounts and categorizes purchases in real time.
- **YNAB (You Need a Budget)**: Links every transaction to your pre-set category limits.
- **Google Sheets API or Tiller Money**: Automatically imports transaction data from your bank into your custom spreadsheet.
- **Shop App** or **Slice**: Tracks orders, shipments, and delivery dates across multiple retailers.

Automating reduces the stress of constant manual entry and helps identify when you're approaching category limits.

Step 5: Verify Discounts and Cashback Credits

During high-volume shopping periods, retailers and cashback programs can make mistakes. Track whether each discount you expected was actually **applied and credited**.

Checklist for verification:

- ◈ Confirm promo code appeared in final total.
- ◈ Compare paid price against your pre-researched target.
- ◈ Check that cashback sites like Rakuten or Honey show pending earnings.
- ◈ Record points or rewards earned on your credit card account.

This ensures that you're not only staying within budget but also maximizing every reward opportunity you earned in Chapter 4.

Step 6: Monitor Delivery and Fulfillment Status

Tracking doesn't stop at checkout—it continues until the product arrives and is verified. Missing packages, incorrect items, or late deliveries can cost both money and time.

Maintain a **Delivery Tracker** within your log:

Order #	Store	Item	Shipped	Estimated Delivery	Delivered	Issue?	Resolution
18274	Walmart	Slow Cooker	11/28	12/2	12/1	No	N/A
45389	Amazon	Vacuum	11/29	12/5	12/4	Missing filter	Requested replacement

Use apps like **Shop**, **Arrive**, or **Parcel** to automatically pull tracking numbers and send alerts when shipments move through checkpoints. This minimizes stress and prevents missed delivery windows.

Step 7: Stay Aware of Refund and Return Windows

Retailers often shorten or complicate return periods during holiday sales. A real-time tracker should flag each purchase's **return deadline** to protect you from expired policies.

Add a column labeled "Return Deadline" in your spreadsheet. Example:

Item	Purchase Date	Return Deadline	Action Needed
Coffee Maker	Nov 28	Dec 14	Test function by Dec 10
Headphones	Nov 29	Jan 10	Gift recipient confirmation pending

Mark calendar reminders or set mobile notifications a few days before each deadline to ensure you don't miss refund opportunities.

Step 8: Track Emotional Spending Triggers

Beyond numbers, smart financial awareness includes **emotional tracking**. Record how you felt when you made each purchase—calm, excited, anxious, impulsive, or satisfied.

This reflection reveals spending triggers that can be refined in future sales. Example notes might include:

- "Felt rushed by timer—almost bought extra accessories."
- "Bought early gift under budget—felt confident."
- "Emotional stress from other errands led to unnecessary impulse buy."

These notes turn your tracker into a **self-awareness journal**, building better discipline for next year.

Step 9: Real-Time Budget Balancing

At the end of each shopping day, total your "Actual Spent" column and compare it against your **budget limits** from Chapter 1.

Formula for quick calculation:

Remaining Budget = Total Budget – Sum(Actual Spent)

Visually represent this with color codes:

- ◈ Green: On or under budget.
- ◈ Yellow: Approaching 85–90% of limit.
- ◈ Red: Over budget; freeze purchases in that category.

If you find one category overspent, adjust by reducing another. For instance, if you went $50 over on gifts, cut $50 from personal indulgences. This keeps your **overall spending neutral** while maintaining control.

Step 10: Track Hidden Costs in Real Time

Black Friday isn't just about sticker prices. Real-time tracking helps catch **hidden expenses** that can quietly drain your funds:

- Shipping upgrades ("Arrives Tomorrow!" fees)
- Subscription trials that start billing later
- Add-on insurance or extended warranties
- Tax and processing fees
- Impulse snacks, gas, or coffee during in-person shopping trips

Record each minor expense under a "Miscellaneous" column. These overlooked costs often total more than one major purchase if left unmonitored.

Step 11: Create an Instant Snapshot Dashboard

For visual clarity, build a **snapshot summary** page that updates in real time. Your dashboard should include:

Category	Budget	Spent	% Used	Status
Gifts	$300	$260	87%	◈ Watch closely
Home	$200	$145	72%	◈ Safe
Personal	$150	$165	110%	◈ Adjust

If you use Google Sheets or Excel, apply formulas to calculate percentages and color rules automatically. This quick-glance overview gives you immediate awareness of spending health without reading every line.

Step 12: Synchronize Across Devices

To truly operate in real time, your tracking system must be **mobile-friendly**. Sync your spreadsheet or app with your smartphone so you can:

- Update on the go while in stores.
- Snap photos of receipts for upload.
- Review totals instantly before checkout.

If you're shopping with a partner or family member, share access so everyone can see live updates and avoid duplicate purchases.

Step 13: Stay Grounded Through Review Moments
Schedule **brief reflection checkpoints** throughout Black Friday:

- Morning: Review totals and delivery updates.
- Midday: Reconfirm remaining budget before continuing.
- Evening: Record all transactions, receipts, and cashback updates.

These mini reviews anchor your awareness and prevent emotional fatigue—the point where shoppers overspend simply from decision exhaustion.

Step 14: Preparing Data for Your Post-Black Friday Review

At the end of the event, export or back up your entire tracker. You'll use it again in **Chapter 6: Post-Black Friday Spending Review** to calculate total savings, evaluate performance, and prepare for next year's improvements.

Be sure to:

- Label your file clearly (e.g., *Black Friday 2025 Tracker – Final Edition*).
- Save both cloud and offline copies.
- Archive all digital receipts and confirmations in a folder with matching names.

This creates a permanent financial record that protects you if issues arise with returns or rebates.

Closing Reflection: Tracking as Empowerment

Tracking in real time is not about restriction—it's about **awareness in motion**. It transforms the chaos of Black Friday into a calm, measurable system where you are always in command.

Each entry in your tracker is a moment of mindfulness. Each total you calculate reinforces financial confidence. And when the weekend ends, you'll look at your log and see not just numbers—but proof of discipline, progress, and control.

You haven't just shopped; you've **strategized your way to financial mastery**.

Chapter 6: Post-Black Friday Spending Review

The Purpose of the Post-Shopping Review

Once the last package arrives and the adrenaline of deal-hunting fades, most shoppers stop tracking their finances — and that's exactly when the *real* savings are determined. True financial success doesn't end at checkout; it begins in reflection.

The **Post-Black Friday Spending Review** is where your planning, budgeting, and tracking merge into insight. This process transforms data into wisdom — showing you what worked, what didn't, and how to prepare for an even stronger, calmer, and more prosperous holiday season.

Your goal in this chapter is threefold:

1. **Reflect** — Examine your emotional and behavioral patterns around spending.
2. **Calculate** — Measure your *true savings* versus perceived savings.
3. **Reset** — Restore your financial equilibrium before the next wave of holiday expenses.

When done correctly, this step turns a shopping event into a financial learning experience that permanently upgrades your money management habits.

Step 1: Gather All Financial Data
Before analyzing, collect every relevant piece of information:

- Your **Real-Time Purchase Tracker** from Chapter 5.
- All **digital and paper receipts**.
- Credit and debit card statements (check for pending transactions).
- Cashback and reward summaries from apps like Rakuten or Honey.
- Emails confirming refunds, returns, or partial credits.

Organize these into a single folder labeled **Black Friday 2025 Review**. This creates a full snapshot of your financial footprint from the event.

Step 2: Verify Final Totals

Once all transactions have cleared your bank, reconcile your budget against your *actual spending*.

Category	Budgeted	Actual Spent	Difference	Notes
Gifts	$300	$285	+$15	Under budget
Home	$200	$215	-$15	Extra décor items
Personal	$150	$120	+$30	Avoided impulse buys
Work	$100	$95	+$5	Discount applied
Miscellaneous	$50	$65	-$15	Shipping upgrades

Now add your columns to calculate:

- **Total Budgeted**
- **Total Spent**
- **Variance (Savings or Overages)**

If your total variance is negative, don't panic — you've identified valuable data on spending pressure points. If it's positive, note what disciplines worked best for replication next year.

Step 3: Calculate Your *True Savings*

A common trap after Black Friday is *perceived savings* — believing you saved more than you did simply because the discount looked large. True savings are measurable and must account for every added cost.

True Savings Formula:

(Regular Price – Final Price Paid) – (Shipping + Taxes + Add-ons)

Example:

- Regular Price: $500
- Final Paid Price: $380
- Shipping: $15
- Taxes: $22

  True Savings = ($500 - $380) - ($15 + $22) = $83

Repeat this for every major item to calculate your **Total True Savings** for the event. You'll often find that the psychological high of "60% off!" might only translate into modest real savings once hidden costs are factored in.

This process creates financial clarity — a foundation of truth that prevents self-deception and promotes awareness.

Step 4: Account for Returns, Refunds, and Adjustments

Many purchases undergo changes after the sale through refunds, exchanges, or price adjustments. Ensure your budget reflects these accurately.

Create a small **Return Log** section:

Item	Store	Refund Amount	Date Processed	Reason	Balance Updated
Headphones	Amazon	$55	12/4	Duplicate order	⟐
Sweater	Macy's	$40	12/10	Wrong size	⟐

If a return is pending, mark it in red until confirmed. Revisit these records weekly until all refunds appear in your account.

Once complete, recalculate your total spending and true savings again for a precise final balance.

Step 5: Review Cashback and Rewards

Your savings journey doesn't stop at refunds — you must also claim and confirm **cashback, rewards points, and rebates.**

Checklist for cashback verification:

- ◈ Rakuten / Honey / Capital One Shopping show pending cashbacks recorded.
- ◈ Credit card reward balances updated correctly.
- ◈ Retailer-specific rewards (Target Circle, Kohl's Cash, etc.) documented with expiration dates.

Pro Tip: Create a **Rewards Tracker Table** with expiration reminders so you can redeem bonuses before they lapse.

Source	Reward Type	Amount	Expiration	Planned Use
Rakuten	Cashback	$18.32	01/10	Holiday food
Visa	Points	3,200	Rolling	Travel fund
Store Credit	Gift Card	$25	12/31	Stocking stuffers

Tracking rewards ensures you collect every dollar of value you've earned — often an overlooked bonus that can fund the next phase of holiday spending.

Step 6: Conduct an Emotional Spending Reflection

Numbers tell you *what* happened; emotions explain *why*.

Spend 15–20 minutes reflecting on how you felt before, during, and after the shopping period. In your planner or journal, answer these prompts:

1. What emotions triggered my biggest impulse purchases?
2. Which buying decisions gave me long-term satisfaction versus short-term excitement?
3. Did I feel more in control compared to previous years?
4. Which strategies helped reduce stress or guilt?
5. What financial boundary felt hardest to maintain?

Documenting emotional responses turns mistakes into measurable lessons. It teaches you where your psychological blind spots appear — whether in time pressure, social comparison, or reward seeking.

Step 7: Identify "Leak Points" in Your Budget

Now analyze *where* overspending occurred and *why*. Leak points often fall into patterns such as:

- **Impulse upgrades** (buying the deluxe version instead of the planned model).
- **Bundle traps** (purchasing extras to "maximize" a deal).
- **Shipping convenience fees** (paying for faster delivery).
- **Duplicate purchases** (buying multiple similar gifts).

Once identified, note what protective strategies you can implement next year. For example:

- Set a "cooling-off timer" before finalizing big purchases.
- Use separate gift and personal funds to avoid emotional overlap.
- Cap daily spending limits instead of total weekend limits.

Each insight becomes a rule for next year's improved budget.

Step 8: Rebalance Your Finances

After the frenzy, take a moment to **re-ground your financial equilibrium**. This involves rebalancing your accounts so the rest of the holiday season remains stress-free.

Action Plan:

1. **Pay off any credit card balances** from Black Friday immediately to avoid interest accumulation.
2. **Move leftover funds** from unused categories (like gifts or décor) into savings.
3. **Recalculate your December cash flow** — update your holiday budget with post-sale figures.
4. **Replenish your emergency fund** if any withdrawals occurred.
5. **Freeze unnecessary spending** for 5–7 days to reset your baseline impulse threshold.

This reset not only restores financial stability but also prepares you mentally for December's ongoing holiday expenses.

Step 9: Celebrate Wins and Growth

A healthy financial mindset thrives on *acknowledged progress*. Recognize every victory, even small ones:

- Sticking to your spending limit.
- Avoiding debt.
- Making informed, guilt-free purchases.
- Maintaining your tracker faithfully.

Celebrate not through another purchase, but through reflection — a coffee outing, journaling moment, or simply revisiting how much calmer this year's experience felt.

By rewarding your discipline, you reinforce sustainable habits that carry into future seasons.

Step 10: Plan for Future Improvement

Use your review insights to create a **"Next Black Friday Strategy Blueprint."** Document:

- What worked perfectly (carry over).
- What went wrong (revise).
- New ideas to test (e.g., prepaid card budgeting, earlier research, team shopping coordination).

Example:

- *Worked:* Category caps and real-time spreadsheet prevented chaos.
- *Needs work:* Forgot to track cashback until late—add automated reminders.
- *Next Year Goal:* Save $200 in advance via a "Holiday Fund Jar."

You're no longer reacting to deals—you're designing mastery over them.

Step 11: Apply Insights to Upcoming Holidays

Your Black Friday review is also your launch pad for the next phase — **December holiday spending**. Take your new clarity and use it to:

- Create an updated **Holiday Gift Budget** using remaining funds.
- Allocate true savings toward seasonal meals, travel, or charitable giving.
- Avoid re-entering "sale mode" by committing to purchase only planned, meaningful items.

By carrying forward your awareness, you maintain a sense of calm control even as year-end pressures rise.

Step 12: Record Final Thoughts in Your Black Friday Spending Journal

Before closing the book on this season, write a final reflection summarizing:

- Total saved vs. total spent.
- Emotional highlights.
- Lessons to remember next year.
- Three habits you're proud of mastering.

This final entry transforms raw financial data into lived wisdom — a personal guide that ensures each Black Friday becomes easier, calmer, and more profitable than the last.

Closing Reflection: The Cycle of Awareness

Your journey began with excitement, continued through structure, and ends in wisdom. The post-Black Friday review is not about judgment; it's about **conscious evolution**. You've proven that mindfulness, data, and reflection can turn consumerism into empowerment.

Every receipt you logged, every impulse you paused, and every dollar you accounted for has strengthened your financial confidence.

This isn't just a planner—it's a mirror of growth. You've transitioned from reactive shopper to **strategic spender**, equipped to face any sale season with composure, clarity, and purpose.

Appendix A: Black Friday Spending Journal

Purpose of the Journal

The **Black Friday Spending Journal** is where your numbers meet your mindset. It's not just a log—it's a mirror that reflects how you interact with money, emotion, and decision-making during one of the most psychologically charged shopping events of the year.

While Chapters 1–6 helped you **plan, execute, and review** your spending strategy, this appendix provides a **dedicated reflective workspace** to record the story behind your transactions. Each page invites you to slow down, observe your thoughts, and translate financial behavior into insight.

Here, you will document:

- Every transaction and its emotional context.
- The patterns behind impulse buys or successes.
- Savings strategies that worked—and those that failed.
- Lessons and affirmations to carry forward into next year's event.

By journaling through the entire Black Friday experience—from anticipation to aftermath—you'll cultivate financial mindfulness that strengthens every purchase decision year-round.

Section 1: Transaction Log — The Factual Record

Use this section to capture **concrete details** about every purchase, return, or refund. It's your master list for financial clarity.

Daily Transaction Entry Template

Date	Store / Platform	Item	Category	Planned Impulse	Budgeted	Actual Cost	Discount %	True Savings	Payment Method	Cashback/ Rewards Earned
11/28	Target	Air Fryer	Home	Planned	$80	$76.49	20%	$3.51	Credit	5% Target Card
11/29	Amazon	Bluetooth Earbuds	Gifts	Impulse	$60	$54.99	10%	$5.01	Debit	2% Rakuten

Date	Store / Platform	Item	Category	Planned or Impulse	Budgeted	Actual Cost	Discount %	True Savings	Payment Method	Cashback/Rewards Earned
11/30	Best Buy	Laptop	Work	Planned	$400	$389	25%	$11	Credit	3% Cashback

◈ **Pro Tip:** Record purchases as soon as they occur. Even a 5-minute delay can cause you to forget emotional context or small additional costs like shipping or tax.

Section 2: Emotional Spending Tracker

Behind every transaction lies an emotion—anticipation, stress, excitement, boredom, or guilt. Mapping these emotions helps you uncover the **psychological patterns** that shape your spending.

◈ Emotional Check-In Log

Date	Purchase	Primary Emotion	Trigger Event	Thought Process	Emotional Outcome
11/28	Air Fryer	Calm, purposeful	Saw ad reminder for planned item	Felt confident because it was pre-budgeted	Satisfaction, no guilt
11/29	Earbuds	Excited, rushed	Limited-time countdown	Bought quickly fearing it'd sell out	Regret after purchase
11/30	Laptop	Focused, strategic	Needed upgrade for work	Compared prices across 3 retailers first	Empowerment, relief

Reflection Prompt:

How often did excitement override logic? Which emotions led to the most confident purchases?

Understanding emotional triggers is the foundation of emotional intelligence in finance. Each time you record one, you weaken its power over future spending decisions.

Section 3: Savings & Strategy Analysis

Use this section to record the *effectiveness* of your financial strategies and deal-hunting techniques. It transforms data into usable feedback for future shopping seasons.

◈ Savings Effectiveness Worksheet

Strategy Used	Result	Notes	Rating (1–5)
Set category budgets in advance	Stayed under total budget	Very effective	◈◈◈◈◈
Used cash-back programs	Earned $23.50 total	Useful, but could optimize timing	◈◈◈◈
Avoided social media ads	Reduced impulse buys	Helped maintain focus	◈◈◈◈◈
Waited 24 hours before unplanned buys	Skipped two unnecessary items	Extremely effective	◈◈◈◈◈
Ignored "Buy More Save More" bundles	Saved money by sticking to list	Difficult but worth it	◈◈◈◈

Analysis Questions:

1. Which of your planned strategies produced the greatest savings or peace of mind?
2. Which tactics failed or felt difficult to maintain under pressure?
3. How can you automate or strengthen successful behaviors next year?

Section 4: Spending Reflection Prompts

Spend quiet time answering these journal prompts to deepen awareness and refine your relationship with money:

◈ Before Shopping (Pre-Event Reflection)

1. What are my top three priorities for this Black Friday?
2. How do I want to *feel* after the event—relieved, proud, guilt-free, in control?
3. What financial mistakes from previous years do I want to avoid this time?

◈ During Shopping (Mid-Event Check-In)

1. Have I stuck to my list so far?
2. Which categories are approaching their limits?
3. What has triggered my strongest buying impulses?
4. Is each purchase improving my life or just my mood?

◈ After Shopping (Post-Event Reflection)

1. Which purchases do I feel the most satisfied with, and why?
2. Which ones triggered buyer's remorse, and what caused it?
3. Did I stay within my financial boundaries?
4. What did this year's experience teach me about my emotional relationship with money?

Write freely — the goal isn't perfection but clarity. Treat this as a safe, judgment-free zone for self-awareness.

Section 5: Post-Event Summary Dashboard

Condense your entire Black Friday experience into a single-page overview. This becomes your quick-reference document next year when preparing for new sales seasons.

◈ Summary Snapshot

Metric	Result	Goal Met?	Notes
Total Budget	$800	◈	Well-planned allocation
Total Spent	$755.48	◈	Stayed within range
True Savings (After Tax & Fees)	$128.72	◈	Verified with receipts
Cashback/ Rewards Earned	$23.50	◈	To be used on holiday groceries
Impulse Buys	2	◈	Emotional triggers identified
Returns Processed	1	◈	Refund completed
Overall Satisfaction	9/10	◈	Calm, strategic, confident

Visual Reminder: Highlight what you're most proud of—discipline, foresight, or improved awareness—so next year's Black Friday feels like an evolution, not a repeat.

Section 6: Lessons for Future Events

Every shopping season should build upon the wisdom of the last. Use this section to summarize insights that will shape your next financial game plan.

◈ Lessons Learned Journal Template

Category	What Worked	What Didn't	Improvement Plan for Next Year
Budgeting	Separate budgets for gifts and personal items kept spending clean	Forgot to include shipping in totals	Add 10% buffer to every category
Emotional Control	Pausing before big purchases reduced guilt	Fell for flash sales mid-day	Set a rule: no unplanned mid-day purchases
Deal Hunting	Comparison research ahead of time paid off	Cashback delays caused confusion	Schedule weekly cashback check-ins
Tracking	Spreadsheet method worked flawlessly	Needed mobile app sync	Use shared Google Sheet next year

Category	What Worked	What Didn't	Improvement Plan for Next Year
Time Management	Started early and avoided panic	Online traffic slowed check-outs	Complete shopping by noon on Friday

At the bottom of each page, write a personal affirmation or mantra for next year:

"My money follows my mindfulness."
"Every purchase I make is a reflection of clarity, not chaos."
"I buy intentionally, save wisely, and end every season empowered."

Section 7: Emotional Debrief — Healing the Consumer Mindset

Black Friday can stir complex emotions — excitement, competition, scarcity, even relief. This final journaling segment helps you release financial tension and reset your energy for the holidays.

Prompt Questions:

1. How do I define *enough* now that the event is over?
2. What did I learn about my relationship to scarcity or abundance?
3. How did I handle social influence—seeing others post their hauls or deals?
4. How do I want to feel about money as I move into the rest of the holiday season?

Reflective note: Gratitude is the antidote to overspending. List three things you're grateful for that money can't buy—peace, time, or connection.

Section 8: Annual Financial Reflection Page

At the end of each year, revisit your spending journals to track your growth. Use this yearly reflection to evaluate how your mindset evolved:

- **Biggest Financial Win:** ___________________________
- **Most Regretted Purchase:** ________________________
- **Top Lesson Learned:** _____________________________
- **Goal for Next Black Friday:** _______________________

This meta-level reflection transforms the planner into a legacy of wisdom — your personal archive of behavioral growth and financial empowerment.

Section 9: Affirmations for Conscious Spending

Conclude your journal with these empowering affirmations to reprogram your shopping mindset:

- "I spend consciously and align every dollar with purpose."
- "Sales are not opportunities to lose money, but moments to practice discipline."
- "I measure wealth not by possessions, but by peace of mind."
- "I trust my ability to plan, track, and make wise financial decisions."
- "Each purchase is a reflection of who I choose to become—mindful, secure, and abundant."

Repeat these affirmations whenever you prepare for future Black Fridays or major sales events.

Closing Reflection: Turning Transactions into Transformation

Your **Black Friday Spending Journal** is more than a ledger—it's a self-awareness ritual. It shows you that money, when managed mindfully, can serve peace instead of anxiety.

Each entry, emotion, and reflection forms a cycle of empowerment:

- You plan with intention.
- You spend with awareness.
- You review with compassion.
- You grow with purpose.

Carry this system into every season that follows. Let it remind you that financial mastery isn't about restriction—it's about freedom through understanding.

With every Black Friday that passes, your journal becomes a chronicle of transformation—a yearly record of how you learned not just to save money, but to *save yourself from overspending*.

Your next step: Revisit this journal at least once a month throughout the holiday season. Reflection turns habit into wisdom—and wisdom turns spending into serenity.

Message from the Author:

I hope you enjoyed this book, I love astrology and knew there was not a book such as this out on the shelf. I love metaphysical items as well. Please check out my other books:

-Life of Government Benefits

-My life of Hell

-My life with Hydrocephalus

-Red Sky

-World Domination:Woman's rule

-World Domination:Woman's Rule 2: The War

-Life and Banishment of Apophis: book 1

-The Kidney Friendly Diet

-The Ultimate Hemp Cookbook

-Creating a Dispensary(legally)

-Cleanliness throughout life: the importance of showering from childhood to adulthood.

-Strong Roots: The Risks of Overcoddling children

-Hemp Horoscopes: Cosmic Insights and Earthly Healing

- Celestial Hemp Navigating the Zodiac: Through the Green Cosmos

-Astrological Hemp: Aligning The Stars with Earth's Ancient Herb

-The Astrological Guide to Hemp: Stars, Signs, and Sacred Leaves

-Green Growth: Innovative Marketing Strategies for your Hemp Products and Dispensary

-Cosmic Cannabis

-Astrological Munchies

-Henry The Hemp

-Zodiacal Roots: The Astrological Soul Of Hemp

- **Green Constellations: Intersection of Hemp and Zodiac**

-Hemp in The Houses: An astrological Adventure Through The Cannabis Galaxy

-Galactic Ganja Guide

Heavenly Hemp
Zodiac Leaves
Doctor Who Astrology
Cannastrology
Stellar Satvias and Cosmic Indicas
Celestial Cannabis: A Zodiac Journey
AstroHerbology: The Sky and The Soil: Volume 1
AstroHerbology:Celestial Cannabis:Volume 2
Cosmic Cannabis Cultivation
The Starry Guide to Herbal Harmony: Volume 1
The Starry Guide to Herbal Harmony: Cannabis Universe: Volume 2
Yugioh Astrology: Astrological Guide to Deck, Duels and more
Nightmare Mansion: Echoes of The Abyss
Nightmare Mansion 2: Legacy of Shadows
Nightmare Mansion 3: Shadows of the Forgotten
Nightmare Mansion 4: Echoes of the Damned
The Life and Banishment of Apophis: Book 2
Nightmare Mansion: Halls of Despair
Healing with Herb: Cannabis and Hydrocephalus
Planetary Pot: Aligning with Astrological Herbs: Volume 1
Fast Track to Freedom: 30 Days to Financial Independence Using AI, Assets, and Agile Hustles
Cosmic Hemp Pathways
How to Become Financially Free in 30 Days: 10,000 Paths to Prosperity
Zodiacal Herbage: Astrological Insights: Volume 1
Nightmare Mansion: Whispers in the Walls
The Daleks Invade Atlantis
Henry the hemp and Hydrocephalus

10X The Kidney Friendly Diet
Cannabis Universe: Adult coloring book

Hemp Astrology: The Healing Power of the Stars

Zodiacal Herbage: Astrological Insights: Cannabis Universe: Volume 2

Planetary Pot: Aligning with Astrological Herbs: Cannabis Universes: Volume 2

Doctor Who: Convergence Protocol – The Replicator War

Nightmare Mansion: Curse of the Blood Moon

The Celestial Stoner: A Guide to the Zodiac

Cosmic Pleasures: Sex Toy Astrology for Every Sign

Hydrocephalus Astrology: Navigating the Stars and Healing Waters

Lapis and the Mischievous Chocolate Bar

Celestial Positions: Sexual Astrology for Every Sign

Apophis's Shadow Work Journal: **:** A Journey of Self-Discovery and Healing

Kinky Cosmos: Sexual Kink Astrology for Every Sign

Digital Cosmos: The Astrological Digimon Compendium

Stellar Seeds: The Cosmic Guide to Growing with Astrology

Apophis's Daily Gratitude Journal

Cat Astrology: Feline Mysteries of the Cosmos

The Cosmic Kama Sutra: An Astrological Guide to Sexual Positions

Unleash Your Potential: A Guided Journal Powered by AI Insights

Whispers of the Enchanted Grove

Cosmic Pleasures: An Astrological Guide to Sexual Kinks

369, 12 Manifestation Journal

Whisper of the nocturne journal(blank journal for writing or drawing)

The Boogey Book

Locked In Reflection: A Chastity Journey Through Locktober

Generating Wealth Quickly:How to Generate $100,000 in 24 Hours

Star Magic: Harness the Power of the Universe

The Flatulence Chronicles: A Fart Journal for Self-Discovery

The Doctor and The Death Moth

Seize the Day: A Personal Seizure Tracking Journal

The Ultimate Boogeyman Safari: A Journey into the Boogie World and Beyond

Whispers of Samhain: 1,000 Spells of Love, Luck, and Lunar Magic: Samhain Spell Book

Apophis's guides:Witch's Spellbook Crafting Guide for Halloween

Frost & Flame: The Enchanted Yule Grimoire of 1000 Winter Spells

The Ultimate Boogey Goo Guide & Spooky Activities for Halloween Fun

Harmony of the Scales: A Libra's Spellcraft for Balance and Beauty

The Enchanted Advent: 36 Days of Christmas Wonders

Nightmare Mansion: The Labyrinth of Screams

Harvest of Enchantment: 1,000 Spells of Gratitude, Love, and Fortune for Thanksgiving

The Boogey Chronicles: A Journal of Nightly Encounters and Shadowy Secrets

The 12 Days of Financial Freedom: A Step-by-Step Christmas Countdown to Transform Your Finances

Sigil of the Eternal Spiral Blank Journal

A Christmas Feast: Timeless Recipes for Every Meal

Holiday Stress-Free Solutions: A Survival Guide to Thriving During the Festive Season

Yu-Gi-Oh! Holiday Gifting Mastery: The Ultimate Guide for Fans and Newcomers Alike

Holiday Harmony: A Hydrocephalus Survival Guide for the Festive Season

Celestial Craft: The Witch's Almanac for 2025 – A Cosmic Guide to Manifestations, Moons, and Mystical Events

Doctor Who: The Toymaker's Winter Wonderland

Tulsa King Unveiled: A Thrilling Guide to Stallone's Mafia Masterpiece

Pendulum Craft: A Complete Guide to Crafting and Using Personalized Divination Tools

Nightmare Mansion: Santa's Eternal Eve

Starlight Noel: A Cosmic Journey through Christmas Mysteries

The Dark Architect: Unlocking the Blueprint of Existence

Surviving the Embrace: The Ultimate Guide to Encounters with The Hugging Molly

The Enchanted Codex: Secrets of the Craft for Witches, Wiccans, and Pagans

Harvest of Gratitude: A Complete Thanksgiving Guide

Yuletide Essentials: A Complete Guide to an Authentic and Magical Christmas

Celestial Smokes: A Cosmic Guide to Cigars and Astrology

Living in Balance: A Comprehensive Survival Guide to Thriving with Diabetes Insipidus

Cosmic Symbiosis: The Venom Zodiac Chronicles

The Cursed Paw of Ambition

Cosmic Symbiosis: The Astrological Venom Journal

Celestial Wonders Unfold: A Stargazer's Guide to the Cosmos (2024-2029)

The Ultimate Black Friday Prepper's Guide: Mastering Shopping Strategies and Savings

Cosmic Sales: The Astrological Guide to Black Friday Shopping

Legends of the Corn Mother and Other Harvest Myths

Whispers of the Harvest: The Corn Mother's Journal

The Evergreen Spellbook

The Doctor Meets the Boogeyman

The White Witch of Rose Hall's SpellBook

The Gingerbread Golem's Shadow: A Study in Sweet Darkness

The Gingerbread Golem Codex: An Academic Exploration of Sweet Myths

The Gingerbread Golem Grimoire: Sweet Magicks and Spells for the Festive Witch

The Curse of the Gingerbread Golem

10-minute Christmas Crafts for kids

Christmas Crisis Solutions: The Ultimate Last-Minute Survival Guide

Gingerbread Golem Recipes: Holiday Treats with a Magical Twist

The Infinite Key: Unlocking Mystical Secrets of the Ages

Enchanted Yule: A Wiccan and Pagan Guide to a Magical and Memorable Season

Dinosaurs of Power: Unlocking Ancient Magick

Astro-Dinos: The Cosmic Guide to Prehistoric Wisdom

Gallifrey's Yule Logs: A Festive Doctor Who Cookbook

The Dino Grimoire: Secrets of Prehistoric Magick

The Gift They Never Knew They Needed

The Gingerbread Golem's Culinary Alchemy: Enchanting Recipes for a Sweetly Dark Feast

A Time Lord Christmas: Holiday Adventures with the Doctor

Krampusproofing Your Home: Defensive Strategies for Yule

Silent Frights: A Collection of Christmas Creepypastas to Chill Your Bones

Santa Raptor's Jolly Carnage: A Dino-Claus Christmas Tale

Prehistoric Palettes: A Dino Wicca Coloring Journey

The Christmas Wishkeeper Chronicles

The Starlight Sleigh: A Holiday Journey

Elf Secrets: The True Magic of the North Pole

Candy Cane Conjurations

Cooking with Kids: Recipes Under 20 Minutes

Doctor Who: The TARDIS Confiscation

The Anxiety First Aid Kit: Quick Tools to Calm Your Mind

Frosty Whispers: A Winter's Tale

The Infinite Key: Unlocking the Secrets to Prosperity, Resilience, and Purpose

The Grasping Void: Why You'll Regret This Purchase

Astrology for Busy Bees: Star Signs Simplified

The Instant Focus Formula: Cut Through the Noise

The Secret Language of Colors: Unlocking the Emotional Codes

Sacred Fossil Chronicles: Blank Journal

The Christmas Cottage Miracle

Feeding Frenzy: Graboid-Inspired Recipes

Manifest in Minutes: The Quick Law of Attraction Guide

The Symbiote Chronicles: Doctor Who's Venomous Journey

Think Tiny, Grow Big: The Minimalist Mindset

The Energy Key: Unlocking Limitless Motivation

New Year, New Magic: Manifesting Your Best Year Yet

Unstoppable You: Mastering Confidence in Minutes

Infinite Energy: The Secret to Never Feeling Drained

Lightning Focus: Mastering the Art of Productivity in a Distracted World

Saturnalia Manifestation Magick: A Guide to Unlocking Abundance During the Solstice

Graboids and Garland: The Ultimate Tremors-Themed Christmas Guide

12 Nights of Holiday Magic

The Power of Pause: 60-Second Mindfulness Practices

The Quick Reset: How to Reclaim Your Life After Burnout

The Shadow Eater: A Tale of Despair and Survival

The Micro-Mastery Method: Transform Your Skills in Just Minutes a Day

Reclaiming Time: How to Live More by Doing Less

Chronovore: The Eternal Nexus

The Mind Reset: Unlocking Your Inner Peace in a Chaotic World
Confidence Code: Building Unshakable Self-Belief
Baby the Vampire Terrier
Baby the Vampire Terrier's Christmas Adventure
Celestial Streams: The Content Creator's Astrology Manual
The Wealth Whisperer: Unlocking Abundance with Everyday Actions
The Energy Equation: Maximize Your Output Without Burning Out
The Happiness Algorithm: Science-Backed Steps to Joyful Living
Stress-Free Success: Achieving Goals Without Anxiety
Mindful Wealth: The New Blueprint for Financial Freedom
The Festive Flavors of New Year: A Culinary Celebration
The Master's Gambit: Keys of Eternal Power
Shadowed Secrets: Groundhog Day Mysteries
Beneath the Burrow: Lessons from the Groundhog
Spring's Whispers: The Groundhog's Prediction
The Limitless Mindset: Unlock Your Untapped Potential
The Focus Funnel: How to Cut Through Chaos and Get Results
Bold Moves: Building Courage to Live on Your Terms
The Daily Shift: Simple Practices for Lasting Transformation
The Quarter-Life Reset: Thriving in Your 20s and 30s
The Art of Shadowplay: Building Your Own Personal Myth
The Eternal Loop: Finding Purpose in Repetition
Burrowing Wisdom: Life Lessons from the Groundhog
Shadow Work: A Groundhog Day Perspective
Love in Bloom: 5-Minute Romantic Gestures
The Shadowspell Codex: Secrets of Forbidden Magick
The Burnout Cure: Finding Balance in a Busy World
The Groundhog Prophecy: Unlocking Seasonal Secrets
Nog Tales: The Spirited History of Eggnog
Six More Weeks: Embracing Seasonal Transitions
The Lumivian Chronicles: Fragments of the Fifth Dimension

Money on Your Mind: A Beginner's Guide to Wealth
The Focus Fix: Breaking Through Distraction
January's Spirit Keepers: Mystical Protectors of the Cold
Creativity Unchained: Unlocking Your Wildest Ideas in 2025
Manifestation Mastery: 365 Days to Rewrite Your Reality
The Groundhog's Mirror: Reflecting on Change
The Weeping Angels' Christmas Curse
Burrowed in Time: A Groundhog Day Journey
Heartbeats: Poems to Share with Your Valentine
Dino Wicca: The Sacred Grimoire of Prehistoric Magick
Courage of the Pride: Finding Your Inner Roar
The Lion's Leap: Bold Moves for Big Results
Healthy Hustle: Achieving Without Overworking
Practical Manifesting: Turning Dreams into Reality in 2025
Jurassic Pharaohs: Unlocking the Magick of Ancient Egypt and Dino Wicca
The Happiness Equation: Small Changes for Big Joy
The Confidence Compass: Finding Your Inner Strength
Whispers in the Hollow: Tales of the Forgotten Beasts
Echoes from the Hollow: The Return of Forgotten Beasts
The Hollow Ascendant: The Rise of the Forgotten Beasts
The Relationship Reset: Building Better Connections
Mastering the Morning: How to Win the Day Before 8 AM
The Shadow's Dance: Groundhog Day Symbolism
Cupid's Kitchen: Quick Valentine's Day Recipes
Valentine's Day on a Budget: Love Without Breaking the Bank
Astrocraft: Aligning the Stars in the World of Minecraft
Forecasting Life: Groundhog Day Reflections
Bleeding Hearts: Twisted Tales of Valentine's Terror
Herbal Smoke Revolution: The Ultimate Guide to Nature's Cigarette Alternative
Winter's Wrath: The Complete Survival Blueprint for Extreme Freezes.

The Groundhog's Shadow: A Tale of Seasons
Burrowed Insights: Wisdom from the Groundhog
Sensual Strings: The Art of Erotic Bondage
Whispered Flames: Unlocking the Power of Fire Play
Forgotten Shadows: A Guide to Cryptids Lost to Time
Six Weeks of Secrets: Groundhog Day's Hidden Messages
Shadows and Cycles: Groundhog Day Reflections
The Art of Love Letters: Crafting the Perfect Message
Romantic Getaways at Home: Turning Your Space into Paradise
Purrfect Brews: A Cat Lover's Guide to Coffee and Companionship
The Groundhog's Wisdom: Timeless Lessons for Modern Life
The Shadow Oracle: Groundhog Day as a Predictor
Emerging from the Burrow: A Journey of Renewal
The Language of Love: Learning Your Partner's Love Style
Authorpreneur: The Ultimate Blueprint for Writing, Publishing, and Thriving as an Author
Weathering the Seasons: Groundhog Day Perspectives
Valentine's Day Magic: A Guide to Romantic Rituals
The Shadow Chronicles: Stories of Groundhog Day
Love and Laughter: Fun Games for Valentine's Day
AstroRealty: Unlocking the Stars for Property Success
The Groundhog's Path: A Guide to Seasonal Balance
Groundhog Day Diaries: Reflections in the Shadow
The Groundhog's Light: Illuminating the Path Ahead
Valentine's Traditions from Around the World
AI Wealth Revolution: Unlocking the Trillionaire Mindset
Love Rekindled: Reigniting Passion in Relationships
Single and Thriving: Self-Love on Valentine's Day
Emerald Legends: Mystical Tales of Ireland
Green Alchemy: Harnessing Nature's Magic
The Hearts of Horror: A Valentine's Day Nightmare

The Leprechaun's Guide to Wealth and Wisdom
Dancing with the Sidhe: Celebrating the Otherworld
Shamrocks and Shadows: Mysteries of the Green Isle
Emerald Energy: Harnessing Luck and Growth
The Gingerbread Golem's Valentine: A Sweetheart's Guide to Love and Enchantment
The Celtic Knot: Weaving Life and Destiny
Green Fire: Elemental Magic for St. Patrick's Day
Clover Chronicles: Finding Your Inner Luck
Ireland's Mystical Creatures: A Field Guide
Gingerbread Golem's Love Almanac
Prowl and Thrive: The Lion's Guide to Success
Love Alchemy: Transforming Your Life Through Heart Energy
WORLD DOMINATION: Woman's Rule 3:The New Life
The Midnight Rose: A Guide to Lunar Love Spells
The Forbidden Letters: Writing Your Own Love Prophecy
Luck and Lore: St. Patrick's Day for Modern Mystics
The Green Path: A Pagan Celebration of Renewal
The Dark Architect's Guide to Reprogramming Reality
Prankster's Paradise: A Guide to Harmless Hijinks
Manifest Your Reality: The Law of Attraction Simplified
The TARDIS Owner's Manual: Understanding the Doctor's Ship: *A complete guide to the TARDIS, its technology, secrets, and mysteries*
Starlit Romance: Astrology Secrets for Finding True Love
The Time Lord's Atlas: A Complete Guide to the Whoniverse: ***A breakdown of the locations, planets, and dimensions explored in Doctor Who***
Sweetheart Shadows: The Dark Side of Love and Attraction
February Fire: Reigniting Passion in Every Area of Life
The Self-Love Toolkit: 5 Ways to Embrace Who You Are
February Sparks: Ignite Your Dreams in 28 Days

March to Success: A 31-Day Action Blueprint
Ancient Paths: The 13 Sacred Principles of Dino Wicca
Echoes of Tomorrow: Navigating the AI Revolution
The Wellness Blueprint: Balancing Mind, Body, and Soul
Green Horizons: Sustainable Living for a Better Tomorrow
The AI Wealth Code: How to Make Millions with Automation
AI-Powered Creativity: Writing, Art, and Music for Profit
Extinction Rites: Rebirthing Your Soul Through Prehistoric Magick
Sacred Serpents tarot
Celestial Enchantment blank journal
Star Strains
Culinary Journeys: Exploring Global Flavors at Home
The Hollowvale Curse
The Hollowvale Harvest
The Egg of Transformation: Awakening Your Inner Power
Blooming Into Power: A Wiccan Guide to Spring Awakening
The Nightmare Nexus: The Third Doctor's Perilous Haunting
Digital Detox: Reclaiming Your Life in a Connected World
Ostara's Path: Walking the Spiral of Renewal
The Sacred Hare
Financial Freedom: Building Wealth in the Modern Age
Spring's Cauldron: Stirring the Waters of Change
The Hollowvale Pact
Quantum Consciousness: The Science of Reality Shifting
The Hollowvale Hunger
The Sacred Waters Within: A Witch's Guide to Hydrocephalus Magick
The Raven's Nest: Building a Life of Unshakable Stability
AI and the Human Mind: The Future of Intelligence
The Hollowvale Reckoning
Timeless Love: Building and Maintaining Lasting Relationships

The Raven's Roar: Unlocking Unstoppable Confidence
Raven Sight: Awakening Intuition and Inner Wisdom
The Butterfly Effect: Small Changes, Big Transformations
Taming the Boogeyman: How to Conquer Your Inner Fears
The Magick of Green: Awakening Earth's Energy in You
The Entrepreneurial Mindset: Secrets to Business Success
The Hollowvale End
The Shadow Luck Ritual: Reclaiming Power from Your Dark Side
Spring Magick for Beginners: A Simple Guide to Seasonal Energy Work
Doctor Who: The Hollowvale Conundrum
The March of Miracles: Unlocking Synchronicities in Spring
Unveiling the Cosmos: A Guide to Stargazing and Space Exploration
The Ultimate Guide to Surviving an Economic Collapse
The AI Gold Rush: How to Profit from the AI Revolution
Bastet's Shadow: The Hidden Power of Feline Magick
The Bastet Codex: Unlocking the Goddess's Magickal Secrets
Purring Spells: Harnessing Bastet's Healing Frequencies
Bastet's Nine Lives: Rebirth, Transformation, and Immortality Spells
Primal Currents: Hydrocephalus Magick in the Path of Dino Wicca
The Digital Gold Rush: Mastering E-Commerce and Online Sales
Future Shock: Adapting to the Next Decade of Change
The Quantum Mindset: Think Like a Billionaire
Sacred Motherhood: Awakening the Divine Feminine Within
The Mother's Spellbook: Enchantments for Love, Protection, and Prosperity
The Witch's Guide to Parenting: Raising Empowered and Intuitive Children

The Magick of Motherhood: Reclaiming Your Power Through Rituals

The Pagan Path to Self-Love: A Goddess's Guide to Worth and Confidence

Wild Woman Magick: Unleashing Your Primal Power

The Money Magnet Blueprint: Unlocking Unlimited Wealth

Biohacking 101: Unlock Your Body's Full Potential

The Wild Father: A Pagan Guide to Strength and Wisdom

The Sacred Masculine: Unlocking Your Inner Power

The Druid's Compass

The Warrior's Mindset

The Father's Fire

Odin's Path

Ancestral Bonds

The House That Whispers

The Magician's Code

The Wild Hunt

The Green Man's Path

The Altar of Success

The Shadow and the Sword

The High Priestess's Guide to Energy Healing

The Lunar Mother

The Sacred Self-Care Grimoire

The Womb Wisdom Codex

The Wheel of the Mother

The Witch's Guide to Manifestation

The Q2 Reset

The Ultimate Guide to AI-Powered Passive Income

Escape the 9-5

AI Feline Fortunes

The Tear-Stained Grimoire

Razorblade Runes

Cemetery Sirens

The Midnight Wristwatch
The Town That Forgets
AI Horror & Creepypasta
The Hollow Frequency
The Breach Echo
The Quiet Between Worlds
The Sigil of Tharan-Khul
Summon the Vault of Y'ha'ten
The Becoming Codex
The Profit of Az'ra-nar
The Drowned Logos
Echoes of the Eldritch Will
The Deep Ledger
Necronomicon of Networth
Covenant of the Wealthwyrm
The Whisperer's Manifesto
The Rites of Azh-K'luth
The Ark of the Crawling Coin
The Tithe of Shadows
Inkheart Abyss
The Timewinds of Y'ha-nthlei
The Spiral Labyrinth of Azag-Nirrh
The Gallifreyan Heresy of the Black Pharaoh
The Psalms of Nyog-Sotha
Black Rain Alchemy
The Infinite Maw
The Entropic Blueprint
The Oracle of Sh'guul
The Book of Breach
The Drowned Saint's Testament
Dreamcraft of the Sleeper God
The Silence Market
Cthonomics: The Dark Wealth Algorithm

Invocation of the Ten-Eyed King
Wealthbound to the Wyrm Below
Become the Unnameable
Codex of the Sovereign Flame
Rituals of Relentless Becoming
The Shadow Ascends
The Eyes Beneath You
The Will That Wakes Worlds
Silence Is a Weapon
The Mirror That Screams
The Whisper Between Moments
The Mind That Devours Fear
The Myth of the Finished Self
The Architect of Your Madness
The Voice You've Buried
The Discipline of Madness
Stormborn: Awakening Your Inner Tempest
The Mind That Ate Time
Unbind Your Becoming
The Pact You Owe Yourself
The Devourer's Diet
The Acid That Carves the Path
The Tower You Must Burn
The Breath Between Worlds
Speak Like the Deep
The Labyrinth Within
The Spine of the Sea God
Rejection Is a Portal
The Crown You Refused
The Scar Is the Spell
The Lightless Flame
The Habit of Becoming Horrific
ChickenJockey Chaos

The Gatekeeper Within
You Are Not Your Name
The Compass of the Mad
The Archive of Unsent Letters
What the Mirror Can't Show You
The Knife You Needed
Worship Nothing, Become Everything
The Other Voice
The Body the World Forgot
The Vein of the Void
The Black Bone Codex
The Puzzle of the Hidden Self (Millennium Puzzle)
The Eye That Sees the Lie *(Millennium Eye)*
The Ring of Return (Millennium Ring)
The Rod of Relentless Will ***(Millennium Rod)***
The Tally of the Soul (Millennium Tauk/Necklace)
The Key to the Locked Timeline (Millennium Key)
The Scale of Sacred Decisions (Millennium Scales)
Inferno Bites: The UnOfficial Minecraft Lava Cookbook
Rot in the Attic
Prana: The Hidden Force of Your Infinite Self
The Shadow Realm Within: Transforming Darkness Into Destiny
The Borderland Collapse
Claws of Protection: Bastet's Defensive Magick
Mr. Ring-a-Ding's Madness
Yugioh Astrology: Celestial Deckcraft and Duel Destiny (2026–2027 Edition)
The Seal You Signed: Unlocking the Power You Once Feared
The Puzzle of Infinite Minds: Unlocking the Mentalism Hidden Within
The Eye That Mirrors the All: Secrets of Inner Reflection
Doctor Who: The Toymaker's Broadcast

The Rod of Eternal Flow: Commanding the Currents of Vibration
Golden Eyes of Bastet: Enhancing Psychic Vision
The Key of Dual Forces: Balance Within the Polarity
The Scales of Living Rhythm: Timing the Dance of Life
The Necklace of Hidden Cause: Weaving the Webs of Fate
The Ring of Secret Masters: Rising Through the All Within All
Daggers of the Dying Deep
Bastet's Wealth and Fortune Magick: Prosperity Rituals of the Goddess
The Tide that Speaks
The Scrolls of Petosiris: 13 Rituals from the Feathered Eye
Petosiris and the Living Plague of Osirion
Feline Fire: Bastet's Passion and Love Magick
The Star Altar of Petosiris
Bastet's Whiskers: Supernatural Sensory Magick
The Bastet Grimoire
Feeding the Shadows
The Mouthless Prayer
The Spiral Wound
Becoming the Ibis: Lessons from Petosiris's Mind
The Crimson Coven: Cola Magick for Sweet Dominion
Sacred Cat's Paw
The Soda Zodiac: A Flavor for Every Sign
Covenant of the Crawling Flame
The Ink of Ish'Zur
Frothroot: The Thirst That Ate the World
The Golden Glyphs of Prosperity
The Etherbind Codex
Echoes of the Resistance: Reclaiming the You That Survived
Harnessed Minds: Breaking Free from Mental Control
The Eyes in the Smoke

Rootwake: The Carbon Covenant
Skitter Logic: Unlearning the Fear That Built You
Doctor Who: The World That Froths
Rootwake: The Fizz That Rewrites Flesh
Rootwake: Frothfather of the World
The Holly Pact: Blood Beneath the Mistletoe
The 2nd Mass Principle: Building Unbreakable Tribes
Web of Wits: A Survival Guide to Encounters with Anasi the Spider (Aunt Nancy)
The Hexbreaking Handbook: Effective Spells to Remove Curses
Pop Alchemy: Transform Your Life One Sip at a Time
The Mason Code: Leading in Unleadable Times
Petosiris and the Fifth Chamber of Thoth
The Ether Seed Within
The Parent of Tomorrow
Petosiris's Pyramid of Perpetual Wealth
Unlearn the World
Grimoire of the Hollow Tongue
Zodiac Weeds: Finding Your Strain Through the Stars
Aquarius Rises in the Bank
The Sugar God's Smile
The Skinclock Reversal: Biohacking the Face of Time
Debtburn: How to Obliterate What You Owe Forever
The Ice Cream Oracle: What Your Cone Says About Your Future
Silence Is Sovereignty: The Power of Being Unreadable
The Wind That Whispers Through Stone
Path of the Four Directions
Doctor Who: The Maestro's Symphony of Endings
Oxygen Grail: Breathing to Undo the Clock
Zodiacal Collapse: When Stars Devour Time
Teachings from the Red Sand Silence

Doctor Who: Omega – The Broken Equation
Memory Wipe Your Past: Start Over Like a MiB
Mitochondria Prime: Ignite the Core of Youth
A Nest of Roaches
Grub from the Galaxy: MiB Recipes You'll Never Forget
Whiskers of Power: Bastet's Guide to Inner Sovereignty
The Gift Must Cost Them: Negotiation Through Unequal Exchange
The Worm Guys' Wealth Code: Hustle Like an Alien
Bug Out: The Edgar Method for Ruthless Goal Setting
Weaving Life with Spiderwoman's Pattern
Doctor Who: The Rani's Renaissance
How to Get a Job (If You're a Puppygirl)
Speak Through Others: The Art of Proxy Power
T-Rex Your Trauma: Reclaim the Power of Your Primal Self
The Black Briefcase: How MiB Stay Wealthy in Silence
The Thirst Beyond Reason: Understanding Diabetes Insipidus From the Inside Out
Backwoods Witchcraft for Billionaires: The Pagan Path from Dirt Roads to Gold Roads
The Moonshine Grimoire: Fermented Spells for Abundance
The Nameless Geometry
The Wraith's Mixtape: Spellcasting with Songs of Sorrow
The Gallifreyan Gentleman: Silent Wealth, Sonic Confidence, and the Doctor's Code of Living
Sugar Water Confidence
Dino Totems: Spirit Guides from Earth's First Gods
Pumpkin Sigils & Ritual Smoke
The Hózhó Compass
The Distortus Discipline – Order from Inner Mutation
Witchcraft for the Cold-Blooded Soul
Moonlight Over the Blessingway
Water, Interrupted: When the Body Forgets How to Hold On

Deformed but Divine: Embracing Your Asymmetry

Hexes in the Henhouse: The Farm Witch's Guide to Power

The Reversed Flame: A Grimoire of Inverted Power

Salt, Cells, and Sanity: Reclaiming Balance with Diabetes Insipidus

King of the Broken: Crowning the Flawed Self

Moonlight Scars: Emo Moon Magick and the Art of Lunar Sorrow

Noose Spells: Magick of the Hanging Rope

The Goth Cathedral: Rituals of the Broken and Beautiful

The Cretaceous Codex: Dino Spirits and Fossil Magick

The Turkey Bones Ritual

Nine Lives of Manifestation: Unlocking Bastet's Reality Codes

Chaos Muscles: Building Strength from Twisted Pain

Emo Blood Magick: The Veins of Power

The 3AM Flood: Nighttime Urination, Sleep Loss, and the DI Spiral

The Silence Between the Stars

The Lemon Method: Sour Your Way to Success

Starlit Sovereign

The Rite of Twelve Gates: Walking the Gates of the Duat.

Cornbread and Conjure: Recipes for Riches and Rootwork

The Black Rose Rituals: Emo Love Spells and Obsession Magick

The Eternal Goodbye: Death Magick and Rebirth Rituals

Sinkrot: The Drain That Remembers

The Hybrid Mindset: Thinking Beyond Evolution

Bone Dry: Navigating Dehydration Before It Breaks You

Wreathcraft: Winter Sigils and Yuletide Spells

The Rite of Twelve Mouths

S'mores of the Damned: Haunted Recipes for Halloween Night

Rethink the Drink: A Beverage Survival Guide for DI Warriors

The Shadow Chord: Guitar Magick and Sonic

Malformed Yet Majestic: Leading When You Feel Wrong Inside

The Cursed Diary: Ink-Stained Spells of the Emo Soul

Anxiety Off Switch: Emergency Reset for a Fried Nervous System

The Energy Heist: How to Take Back Your Life from Drainers

Beyond the Bathroom: Rebuilding Your Social Life With DI

Coyote's Gift for Decision Makers

Ghoul-Goo: Spooky S'mores You'll Die For

Echoes in the Mirror: Scrying and Self-Destruction Magick

Thread and Thorn: Stitching Spells from Rural Cloth

The Mogwai Mind: Building Untouchable Wealth from Small Ideas

Be Your Own Guide: Trust Your Inner Compass

Hormones in Chaos: The Endocrine Puzzle of Diabetes Insipidus

ChronoCleanse: Detox Your Biological Timeline

The Limb You Hide Is the One That Saves You

Leaves, Bones, and Whisper Spells

The Dinosaur Mindset: Prehistoric Tactics for Modern Wealth

Clawing Back Control: A Bastet Method for Boundaries and Empowerment

Samhain Codes of the Forgotten

Orange Alchemy: The Autumnal Spellbook

Monster Within, Master Without

The Sigil That Sleeps

Hearthcraft: Yule Hearth Sigils and Winter Warmth Spells

Temple of the Purring Moon: Rituals from Bastet's Lineage

When the Earth Remembers Your Footsteps

Food for Mood: Eat to Heal Depression, Not Just Survive It
Witch of the Kudzu Vine: Southern Pagan Wealth Secrets
The Invisible Diagnosis: Advocating for Yourself With DI
The Coffin's Lullaby: Sleep Magick and Nightmares as Portals
Ashes of the Will: Rituals for Erasing the Self
The Fracture Rite: Shattering the Magickal Core
Funeral Candles: The Art of Emo Flame Magick
The Black Grimoire: A Blank Ritual for Writing in Absence
Phantom Thirst: A Halloween Survival Guide for Diabetes Insipidus
The Hollow Crown: Emo Royalty and Magick of the Outcast King
Sandpainting for the Soul
Falling Into Balance: Using the Extra Hour to Recalibrate Life
100 Southern Superstitions That Still Work
The DI Child: A Parent's Guide to Raising Hydrated, Happy Kids
The Jungle of Shame: Escaping the Hidden Lab of Doubt
The Witch's Toast: S'mores Spells and Creepy Confections
The Hoodoo Pantry: Spells from the Mason Jar
The Immortal Fortune: Secret Wealth Lessons from Captain Jack Harkness
The Specter's Embrace: Magick for Channeling Ghostly Lovers
Grateful Waters: A Thanksgiving Survival Guide for Diabetes Insipidus
The Seizure Gospel
Harvestbind: Autumn Sigils and Samhain Spells
Doctor Who: The Algorithmic Awakening
Silent Nights, Steady Waters: A Christmas Survival Guide for Diabetes Insipidus
The Extra Hour Effect: How One Hour Can Transform Everything

Blade Between the Breaths

Running with the Mountain Shadows

Echoes of the Failed Experiment – Becoming a Living Legacy

Swamp Witches & River Ghosts: Real Southern Hauntings

Cornbread Prophecies: Magical Recipes from a Southern Table

Doctor Who: The Signal in the Star

Bloomcraft: Spring Sigils and Equinox Enchantments

Vanisher: How to Disappear from the Internet Without Losing Your Life

The Ultimate Christmas Cookie Cookbook

The Unbreakable Parent: How to Mentally Survive Raising Kids in a Broken World

Time Debt: How to Reclaim the Hours You Didn't Know You Lost

One Month, One Million: Unconventional Cash Creation Tactics

Doctor Who: The Cyber Conversion Protocol

Black Friday Frenzy: The Art of Finding Hidden Online Deals

The Grimoire Buried Under the Apple Tree

Digital Couponing Masterclass: Your Step-by-Step Guide to Black Friday Savings

The Fire Inside the Flint

Shadows on the Ceiling: The Emo Guide to Astral Magick

The Bone-Eaters Beneath Us

Black Friday Bundle Blueprint: Creating Irresistible Product Packages for Maximum Sales

Thirteen Nights of Unbinding

Doctor Who: Engines of Influence

Pumpkin Spice Alchemy: Recipes of Fire and Frost

When Raptor Met Rexy: Prehistoric Lessons in Wild Romance

Oblivion's Candle: Burn the Path Behind You

Campfire Curses and Chocolate: A Halloween S'mores Grimoire

The Wallet That Wasn't Mine: Breaking Free from Inherited Scarcity

The Cola Zodiac: What Your Fizz Says About Your Fate

Frostfire Fortune: Unlocking Winter's Hidden Prosperity

Signal Jamming: Detox Your Brain from Info Overload

The Dust of the Forgotten Rite

The Golden Cat Sigils: Drawing Power in Bastet's Name

Mud Magick: The Prosperity of Getting Dirty

Savory Spicefall: Beyond the Pumpkin Pie

Pumpkin Spice Apothecary Kitchen

The Pumpkin Spice Economy: Turning Trends into Billions

The Ember Veil: 13 Nights of Fire Magick

Financial Freeze: When Earning Triggers Panic

The Gingerbread Alchemist: Sweet Recipes with a Twist

Biosynth Power: Programming Yourself from Scratch

Echoes from the Talking Circle

Truffle Alchemy: Fungus of Fortune

Spores of Power: The Truffle Witch's Handbook

Doctor Who: The Tower That Speaks

The Mycelium Veil: Truffle Magick Unbound

Broke But Ashamed: Healing the Shame Wound of Debt

The Evergreen Mind: Growth Through Winter Stillness

The Black Veil Truffle Rite

The Voice Beneath Symbols

Witchlight on the Bayou: Swamp Spells for Sovereignty

I Grew Up Poor and Now I Sabotage My Success

The Lantern of Hollow Souls

Shutdown Survival: A Citizen's Guide to Thriving When Government Stops

When Abundance Feels Like a Threat: Healing the Hidden Fears of Enough

The Scarecrow Grimoire
Owls of the October Veil
Candlewax and Curses: A Halloween Spellbook
Excavating the Inner Fossil – Transforming Fossilized Thoughtforms into Tools of Power
The Yule Witch's Spellbook: Magick for the Holiday Season
Haunted Christmas: Ghost Stories for Winter Nights
The Christmas Survival Guide: Thriving Through the Chaos
The Bone Orchard Rites
Haunted Commerce: The Ghost in the Marketplace
When Money Triggers the Inner Child
Silent Night with the Silence: A Christmas Thriller
The Lightning Crown: Living and Leading Through Seizures
TARDIS Tidings: Festive Stories from the Whoniverse
Autumn Reset: Slowing Down Without Falling Behind
The Trillion Dollar Soul: Rewriting the Currency of Reality
Truffle Eclipse Magick
Micro-Manifestations: Quick Magick That Works
5-Minute Rituals for Busy Witches
The Marshmallow Massacre: Halloween Treats with a Sinister Twist
Blood and Blackberry Thorns
Magickal Mornings: Rituals for a Blessed Christmas Day
Embers of the All-Hallows Fire
The Pumpkin Market Collapse
The Hour You Gained: Transforming Time Into Power
The Chamber Must Be Sealed: Mastering the Power of Controlled Access
The Cursed Manuscript of Petosiris
The Festive Hearth: Creating Holiday Traditions
Darkness Rising: Thriving as Nights Grow Longer
Harvesting Time: Turning the Year's End Into Your New Beginning

Petosiris and the 13th Zodiac Key
Wagewound: When Paychecks Become Identity Prisons
Walls That Watch
The Silent Feast: Rituals of Power in the Longest Night
The Distortus Legacy : Becoming a Deformed King in a Perfect World
The Hollow Masks
The Gratitude Furnace: Forging Gold from Thanks
Feast of Inner Gold: Eating for Energy and Enlightenment
Haunted Commerce: The Season of Spending Spirits
Fear Bonds: How Panic Creates Profit
Black Friday E-Commerce Playbook: Sales Tactics to Skyrocket Your Holiday Revenue

Get Some Tarot cards: https://www.makeplayingcards.com/sell/apophis-occult-shop

Get some shirts: https://www.bonfire.com/store/apophis-shirt-emporium/

Instagrams:
@apophis_enterprises,
@apophisbookemporium,
@apophisscardshop
Twitter: @apophisenterpr1
Tiktok:@apophisenterprise
Youtube: @sg1fan23477
Hive: @sg1fan23477
CheeLee: @SG1fan23477

Podcast: Apophis Chat Zone: https://open.spotify.com/show/5zXbrCLEV2xzCp8ybrfHsk?si=fb4d4fdbdce44dec

Newsletter: https://apophiss-newsletter-27c897.beehiiv.com/

If you want to support me or see posts of other projects that I have come over to: **buymeacoffee.com/mpetchinskg**

I post there daily several times a day

Get your Dinowicca or Christmas themed digital products, especially Santa Raptor songs and other musics. Here: **https://sg1fan23477.gumroad.com**

Apophis Yuletide Digital has not only digital Christmas items, but it will have all things with Dinowicca as well as other Digital products.

www.ingramcontent.com/pod-product-compliance
Lightning Source LLC
LaVergne TN
LVHW022228200926
848481LV00006B/2178
9798349621093